THE DALAI LAMA
IN WOODSTOCK

THE DALAI LAMA
IN WOODSTOCK

Celebrating

The United Nations International Day of Peace

Thursday, September 21, 2006

KTD Publications
Woodstock, New York

A tremendous gift
to the town of
Woodstock.

Jeremy Wilber
Town Supervisor of Woodstock

Published by:
KTD Publications
335 Meads Mountain Road
Woodstock, NY 12498, USA
www.KTDPublications.org

Photographs by Robert Hansen-Sturm: ii-iii (all sky images), iv-v, xi, xx, xxiii, xxxiv, 2-3, 7, 12-13, 15, 17, 21, 23, 29, 31, 35, 41, 43, 45, 46-47, 50-51, 55, 59, 60-61, 68, 70.
Photographs by Andrea Barrist Stern: xiv, xxviii, 11, 24-25, 33, 57, 59, 63, 64, 66-67.

Woodstock dove logo: TM WOODSTOCK VENTURES LC: WOODSTOCK® is a registered trademark of Woodstock Ventures, LC and is used pursuant to a License Agreement with Woodstock Licensing, LC.

Contents

Foreword
by Tashi Wangdi

His Holiness the Dalai Lama always speaks to people about the importance of kindness, love, and compassion. Spoken with simplicity, humor, and great warmth, his message is the same for everyone—we all want to be happy and in order to accomplish this happiness it is important to develop and nurture a compassionate and open state of mind.

This little book commemorating His Holiness the Dalai Lama's visit to the Town of Woodstock, on the United Nations International Day of Peace, September

21, 2006, will serve as a reminder to the people of Woodstock, and their friends and neighbors, about the importance of the universal values of love, compassion, and warmheartedness.

We hope that the publication of this book will help to facilitate His Holiness' wish for a compassionate human society based on religious tolerance, happiness for all, and world peace.

Mr. Tashi Wangdi
Representative of His Holiness the Dalai Lama
The Office of Tibet, New York, New York

His Holiness the Dalai Lama:
A Short Biography
by Michele Martin

His Holiness the Fourteenth Dalai Lama, Tenzin Gyatso, is the spiritual and temporal leader of the Tibetan people. On July 6, 1935, he was born into a peasant family living in a small village called Taktser in northeastern Tibet. Following Tibetan tradition, he was recognized at the age of two as the reincarnation of his predecessor the Thirteenth Dalai Lama. The Dalai Lamas are considered to be the manifestations of Chenrezik, the Bodhisattva of Compassion, whose only intention is to benefit others. The Dalai Lama's name means Ocean of Wisdom.

suppressions of the Tibetan national uprising by Chinese military forces failed, His Holiness escaped to India where he was given political asylum. In all, 80,000 Tibetans followed him into exile. Since 1960 he has resided in Dharamsala, the seat of the Tibetan Government-in-Exile. He remains firmly committed to the path of nonviolence and to finding a solution for the Tibetan issue through negotiations and understanding.

In 1963, His Holiness promulgated a democratic constitution, based on Buddhist principles and the Universal Declaration of Human Rights, as a model for a future free Tibet. For decades, he has set up educational, cultural, and religious institutions which have made great strides in preserving Tibet's identity and rich heritage.

Since 1967, His Holiness has journeyed to more than forty nations. His reputation as a scholar and man of peace has grown steadily. In recent years, a number of universities and institutions have conferred peace awards and honorary doctorate degrees upon His Holiness. In October 2006, he received the Congressional Gold Medal, the highest civilian honor in the United States. The ceremony will be held in October 2007. In November 2006, he received the Honorary Citizenship of Canada, one of the highest national awards given to a foreign leader.

In 1989, he was awarded the Nobel Peace Prize. In its citation, "the committee wants to emphasize the fact that the Dalai Lama in his struggle for the liberation of Tibet has consistently opposed the use of violence. He has instead advocated peaceful solutions based upon tolerance and mutual respect in order to preserve the historical and cultural heritage of his people. The Dalai Lama has developed his philosophy of peace from a great reverence for all things living and upon the concept of universal responsibility embracing all mankind as well as nature."

His Holiness always speaks of his belief in the oneness of the human family and the need for each individual to develop a genuine sense of universal responsibility, of the commonality of faiths and the need for unity among different religions, and of love and compassion as the moral fabric of world peace.

"I am just a simple Buddhist monk—no more, no less." Following the life of a Buddhist monk, His Holiness lives in a small cottage in Dharamsala. He rises at four in the morning to meditate and pursues a busy schedule of administrative meetings, private audiences, and religious teachings and ceremonies. He concludes each day with further prayer before retiring. In explaining his greatest sources of inspiration, he often cites a favorite verse, found in the writings of the renowned eighth-century Buddhist saint Shantideva:

> For as long as space endures
> And for as long as living beings remain,
> Until then may I too abide
> To dispel the misery of the world.

The United Nations International Day of Peace

September 21

According to the United Nations resolution declaring September 21 as the International Day of Peace, it is a day that "should be devoted to commemorating and strengthening the ideals of peace both within and among all nations and peoples." So it is particularly fitting that His Holiness the Dalai Lama, winner of the 1989 Nobel Peace Prize, visited Woodstock on this day commemorating peace in all its myriad forms.

The International Day of Peace first began twenty-five years ago. As stated in the original United Nations General Assembly resolution, its purpose is "...to devote a specific time to concentrate the efforts of the United Nations and its Member States, as well as of the whole of mankind, to promoting the ideals of peace and to giving positive evidence of their commitment to peace in all viable ways." In 2006, all member states of the UN pledged themselves to a global cease-fire and a day of nonviolence.

The Town of Woodstock and its Tibetan Buddhist monastery, Karma Triyana Dharmachakra (KTD), together with His Holiness the Dalai Lama were honored to participate in this worldwide celebration of peace and nonviolence, ideals at the heart of His Holiness' message.

Tashi Delek
by Jeremy Wilber

I have been asked what it was like to receive His Holiness the Dalai Lama during his visit to Woodstock in September, and to have received his blessing following the conclusion of the teaching he gave to the 2,500 townspeople who came to listen.

It was a perfect September afternoon. The Dalai Lama arrived in a motorcade. He is immediately recognizable, and when I saw him through the window I took a step toward him. A suited gentleman in the front seat gave me a look that said, "Take one more step and I will blow your head off," and had he shown much less, I think I still would have frozen, even during that seasonably warm moment. All the cars stopped. Several doors shuddered open at precisely the same moment and several suited agents of the Diplomatic Security Service alighted with their right hands poised inside their left lapels. They all made 360-degree surveys. One nodded. Another opened the door for a man who still does not seem to recognize the necessity of all this. He had the expression an exceptionally beautiful child might have when yet another grownup insists on fussing over him.

I stood with a khatak draped over my extended arms, having almost lost my wits trying to unravel it to properly place it over my arms. It had taken the feverish help of

both my assistants to untangle it just moments before the motorcade arrived.

"Tashi delek," I said in my rough-hewn Tibetan, while offering the khatak.

He returned the greeting, took the khatak from me, pressed it to his lips, and placed it around my shoulders.

"There are so many who await you," I gabbled, expecting him to be swallowed by the phalanx of suits and escorted to the stage that had been beautifully decorated for him. He said words to the effect, "Let's go then," and taking my hand we walked together to the field.

On the stage His Holiness bowed while many, many cameras earned their keep. It was then my privilege to introduce him.

I said to the townspeople, "On your behalf I say to our guest:

Te ring dir pep bar ka trin chay
Je ma yang yang pep rog nang.

Thank you for coming today.
We hope you will come back again and again.

When His Holiness had finished the forty-five minute teaching he turned to me and thanked me for my attempt to greet him in his native Tibetan. He then presented his khatak to me, wrapped it around my shoulders, and then took my head into his hands, pressed his forehead to mine and looked deeply.

In particular, people have asked me what that was like. I can only offer an analogy:

In 1981 I was working in Lake Granby, Colorado. On Friday nights the two carpenters I worked with and I would pile into the car and drive to Longmont. On the way we would pass the Rocky Mountain Arsenal where they made nuclear triggers. Standing in front of the fence was a young Japanese Zen monk holding a sign that said "Peace." Not terribly remarkable except that it was ten degrees out and he wore nothing but a smock and slippers. He didn't shiver; he just stood there casually. When we drove back on Sunday night, there he was again, same composure. Every week we witnessed this.

Without trying to explain life's surprises, in April of

that year I drove this very same monk to Los Angeles. He was about twenty, and spoke no English. As we approached the New Mexico desert the sun began to set. The monk began a chant that sounded as old as the crags that we passed. A secret of the universe unveiled itself, and although I got a solid glimpse I could no more tell you what I saw than I could explain rainbows to the blind.

That's my story. I would only add that, after thinking about it, I believe His Holiness was blessing all of us. I have never seen the people in my town so open to such a positive message. I'm sure that His Holiness appreciated it. So really, to those of you who asked me—what was it like for you?

Jeremy Wilber
Town Supervisor, Woodstock, New York

Genuine Compassion
by Andrea Barrist Stern

The best-kept "secret" in Woodstock, New York for a very long time—possibly ever—was the Dalai Lama's public talk at Andy Lee Field at 3:45 p.m. on Thursday, September 21, 2006, news of which had circulated as intended in the weeks before only by word-of-mouth to ensure a manageable crowd would gather.

Speaking for slightly under an hour to approximately 2,500 people—most of them from the local area—on a stage that had been erected that morning so as not to let word of the planned event escape, His Holiness the

Fourteenth Dalai Lama, Tenzin Gyatso, the head of the Tibetan government-in-exile, spiritual leader of the Tibetan people, and 1989 Nobel Peace Prize winner brought his message of compassion, tolerance, and forgiveness to Woodstock on what was the United Nations International Day of Peace.

After donning a microphone headset that seemed incongruous with his monk's robes, the Tibetan leader opened by pointing to the Woodstock Cemetery that adjoins the field, chortling with laughter, "That's the final destination." Before reaching that point, however, we should spend our lives having a "meaningful life," one that brings happiness to both ourselves as well as to others.

The remarks constituted a basic lesson in what the

Buddhist teacher referred to as "genuine compassion." It is this kind of compassion that leads to better communications with others and, ultimately, one's own happiness, he stressed. "We all have the right to a successful, happy life," said the Dalai Lama, whose simple message of human decency could be understood on many levels.

Clearly able to appreciate his own stories as much as his listeners and devotees, the Dalai Lama erupted with laughter on several occasions, including his memory of a parrot he had as a young boy at the palace in Lhasa, where he grew up among monks. His Holiness admitted having been jealous of the parrot's devotion to a particular monk. The audience roared when the Dalai Lama admitted he had even been a little rough with the bird. This in a small town so attuned to animal rights issues that it has its own farm animal sanctuary and numerous animal rescue groups and where, only half an hour before, the audience had applauded the German Shepherd bomb dog brought in to do a security sweep.

"My relationship with that parrot got much worse," the Dalai Lama continued, shaking with mirth by this point. "Like humans, animals know whether affection is genuine or not," he said. "True affection leads to tolerance, forgiveness, and happiness," he added, pointing to his own life, which, he said, had been shaped by many "sad things," including his experience as a refugee.

Following these remarks, the Dalai Lama and his entourage traveled up Meads Mountain Road past lines of traditional Tibetan prayer flags and several homemade banners that had been hung out by residents in honor of the occasion, including one that read "Hello Dalai."

The Buddhist leader who refers to himself as a "simple monk," rising each morning at 4 a.m. to do 108 prostrations to the Buddha before performing his prayers and meditating for four hours, left the next day, promising to return after KTD's new monastery building is completed. KTD is the North American seat of His Holiness the Seventeenth Gyalwa Karmapa, Ogyen Trinley Dorje, head of the Karma Kagyu School of Tibetan Buddhism.

Andrea Barrist Stern
from the Woodstock Times
October 2, 2006

Bodyguard Embodies
Courage and Compassion
by Lama Kathy Wesley

Standing at the left hand of the Dalai Lama, about ten feet from his brocaded throne, was a man who could have been any mother's son. Six feet tall, trim, and clean-cut, his short but well-groomed black hair matching his dark suit, he stood attentive, brown eyes scanning the crowd of 2,500 people, waiting for some flash of movement betraying untoward intentions.

He was serious, a sentinel, a man who, despite his casual, unbuttoned white shirt, was serious and alert. This young agent of the State Department's Diplomatic

Security Service would die at any moment, willingly, for the man sitting on the throne. Tears welled in my eyes as I considered this possibility.

The Dalai Lama is said to be Chenrezik, the Bodhisattva of Compassion, whose altruism is legendary in the Buddhist world. And yet, at this moment, it was not that knowledge that made me cry. It was the realization that this young man's life could end in a moment, as he dove in front of an assassin's bullet to save the Dalai Lama.

The man was carefully taught to sacrifice his life for a higher ideal. Every step of that path—learning how to spot danger in a milling crowd, how to hold and shoot a gun, how to seem invisible and very present at the same time—was leading his warrior's soul to a hero's funeral.

This young agent of the Diplomatic Security Service would die at any moment, willingly, for the man sitting on the throne. Tears welled in my eyes as I considered this possibility.

Yes, that was it. A warrior. Willing to end his life to save another's. And what did I have in my life that I would be willing to die for?

It is said that when Chenrezik was an ordinary man, he stood before a Buddha and took the Bodhisattva Vow, promising to work for the benefit of all the suffering beings in this world, always putting others first, until all are liberated.

When Chenrezik took his vow, he added an important stipulation. Until all beings had been liberated from suffering, he said, he himself would stay in the world of suffering, working to free them. It is said that when he did this, all those in the assembly bowed toward his courage, honoring what they themselves could not attempt.

So it was that this young agent touched my heart. Standing on the left hand of the man said to be the embodiment of Chenrezik's compassion in this world, he was both the compassion of Chenrezik and the courage I someday hope to achieve.

Lama Kathy Wesley
KTD Faculty Member and
Resident Lama of the Columbus KTC
(Karma Thegsum Chöling)
Written at KTD, September 21, 2006

This book is dedicated to His Holiness the Fourteenth Dalai Lama

May your life be excellent,
May your life be long,
May all your aspirations be fulfilled.

TM Woodstock Ventures LC

THE DALAI LAMA SPEAKS
TO THE PEOPLE OF WOODSTOCK

At the invitation of Karma Triyana Dharmachakra, His Holiness the Dalai Lama visited Woodstock on September 21, 2006, the day designated by the United Nations as the International Day of Peace. He was introduced to a crowd gathered at Andy Lee Field by town supervisor Jeremy Wilber, who thanked KTD for what he called a "tremendous gift to the town of Woodstock." Mr. Wilber then addressed His Holiness with these words in Tibetan:

TE RING DIR PEP BAR KA TRIN CHAY
JE MA YANG YANG PEP ROG NANG.

Thank you for coming today.
We hope you will come back again and again.

Hello! Tashi Delek! It's a beautiful, sunny day, and we are sitting in a field surrounded by a beautiful forest and small, tidy houses. It's really very beautiful, very tidy. Over there, in the cemetery next to this field, is our final destination. Before reaching there, we have a life span of about a hundred years at most, and I believe that period should be utilized to live a meaningful life. A meaningful life means that you are happy yourself and that you bring happiness to other people and create a happier, peaceful environment. That is what I think is meaningful. Therefore, wherever I go there are two things that I always share with others. Number one, we are all sentient human beings, and we all have every right to have a successful, happy life. Particularly in the West, where society is more affluent, people generally consider a successful life to mean more prosperity, more money, more fame. They think that material facilities are the means to success. However, if that were the case, then individuals who already have material facilities—money, friends, fame, power—should be one hundred percent happy. But that's not the case. I have rich friends in Europe and here in America, and in Japan and India as well. They may be rich, but as persons they are sometimes very unhappy. Sometimes they have a lonely feeling, sometimes suspicion and doubt. Always there is something else that we want, there is some restless feeling. This clearly shows that a truly happy and peaceful mind does not depend entirely on external or material things. On the other hand, among people who have just a

few material facilities but no luxuries, there are some who are really happy. They worry very little, and even when something happens, they face their difficulties more easily. This shows that it is a mistake to place too much trust in external means, and to allow our hopes and expectations to rely on material goods. We should never forget or neglect our inner values. By inner values I mean feelings of closeness or human affection, in other words, human compassion. Human compassion is the main component of our inner values, and this is the second point that I always share with people. I call these things human values because they come not from religious faith or civil laws or education, but by birth. We are born with these qualities already present, and in fact, without feelings of affection and closeness we cannot survive. For example, just after you are born you see another person. You have no idea who that person is, but biologically you must completely rely on the person who is caring for you, and that is usually your mother. From the mother's side comes a tremendous sense of caring and concern, and a feeling of closeness. That person, our mother, treats us as even more precious than her own life. The more nurturing and warm feelings that the child receives from its mother, the more the child grows up well and healthy. We can observe that children are much happier when they come from a warm family full of love and affection, and they are physically healthier as well. Mentally they are fresher; they show interest in many things and because of that they learn

We should never forget or neglect our inner values. By inner values I mean feelings of closeness or human affection, in other words, human compassion.

quickly and in a variety of ways. Proper development on both physical and mental levels is more difficult for children who grow up in a family that is cold, with little love and affection, and it is even worse when there is fear as a result of abuse or trauma. Such children usually exhibit more anger, hatred, and fear, and these negative emotions become dominant. I think that in order to learn the value of human goodness, you don't need to read many books—you just need to look. We can judge from our own experience. If someone gives you an expensive present, but does so with a cold look on their face, you will not feel happy. A precious stone may make a silly person feel happy, but I think a sensible person will prefer something smaller, even a cheap gift, if it is given with warm feeling.

That's really the wonderful quality of human beings, that from birth we have this kind of warmheartedness, this love and affection.

Maybe that small gift is just a little more precious than the expensive one. Whenever we meet people who smile at us with genuine feeling, and without suspicion, we feel very happy. But we don't like to see someone who always looks a little stern, or whose smile seems artificial. I think that not only humans, but also animals—dogs, cats, birds— respond very nicely if we feed them with sincere feeling. In 1959 when I left Tibet, I had a dog that I had to leave behind. I did not feel bad about that, because my relationship with the dog was not very good. You see, although I wanted a friendly attitude from the dog, my own attitude was sometimes kind and sometimes a little prone to disciplinary actions. As a result that dog, who was quite smart, was sometimes nice to me and sometimes not nice, and I did not think he had a very friendly attitude. At another time when I was very young, I had a small parrot. One of my attendants, an old monk, whenever he was passing through, fed nuts to that bird. The parrot got excited whenever he heard the old man's footsteps, even from a distance, and when the monk fed him he was delighted and affectionate. Then I got to thinking, "The real owner of that parrot is me, not that monk." I wanted my parrot to have a good attitude toward me, too, so I fed him nuts a few times. He had been so nice to the monk, but when I gave him a nut, he would take it and eat it, and then peck at me aggressively. Eventually I lost my temper, and I used a little stick to punish him. In the end my relation with that small parrot worsened; it got much worse, with no hope of reconciliation. So that's the story. The point is that those animals, poor animals, appreciate genuine affection, and they also know if a person is cheating or tricking them. They know. They have no religion, no constitution—nothing, no police—but they do appreciate genuine affection. That's really the wonderful quality of human beings, that from birth we have this kind of warmheartedness, this love and affection. I think that another reason for this is that a human being is basically a social animal. After all, the survival of a child entirely depends on someone else's care. Because of that reality, there is a certain emotional element that bonds us together—that creates the bond between individuals, between mother and child, and between the community and individuals. If

a person neglects these things, they will eventually suffer, and suffer a lot. It is clear that if we neglect these values in the family and in the community, then we will not have happy families or a happy society. That is the fundamental thing about a happy life, and in fact I think it is the fundamental basis of our life. You see, once genuine love and affection are there, then the spirit of forgiveness comes and tolerance also comes. Contentment, self-discipline, and not harming others do not come out of fear of the law. It's not like that. Another person is just like me and does not want to suffer, and that is why I should not harm him. If I harm that person, then essentially I have lost a potential friend. That's the way it is. All other values—including justice, honesty, and truthfulness—come

from human warmheartedness, and that is why I sometimes call it a universal religion. It is the universal value, so we should think about it and try to keep these inner qualities above all else. I want to share this philosophy and belief because it benefits me as well. In my life I have passed through many difficulties and many different circumstances. I am still passing through these things. I am still a refugee, and there is still a lot of sadness there. Nevertheless, my own experience tells me that these inner qualities give me inner strength. The more inner strength you have, the easier it is to face challenges. When challenges come, instead of losing hope you will become more determined and you will have more willpower. The practice of compassion really gives you inner strength, and as a result, you have less fear. With a more compassionate heart, it is easier to communicate with other people because your outlook toward others is positive. If their attitude becomes negative in spite of your positive attitude, then of course you have the right to judge what kind of appropriate measure is necessary. But first of all, from your own side, reach out and create a positive environment, and that will produce a happy atmosphere. I want to make it clear that there are usually different levels of what we call compassion. You feel compassion toward your own friend or loved one, and that kind of compassion is mixed with attachment. Another kind of compassion is more a feeling of pity, with an element of looking down on another person. You feel superior, so there is no sense of equality or

You see, once genuine love and affection are there, then the spirit of forgiveness comes and tolerance also comes.

respect. Both of these kinds of compassion are biased. Genuine compassion is to consider another to be just like you. On that basis you respect the other person and you respect their rights, and then you develop a sense of concern when they are passing through difficulties. You feel compassion for the other person irrespective of what their attitude is toward you—whether they are a friend or an enemy or a neutral person. That kind of compassion can reach all types of people, and that is the real compassion. Now how do we develop real compassion? First of all, we already have the seed of compassion from birth. All human beings, including past dictators or merciless leaders such as Hitler or Stalin, as babies had the same experience with their mothers—the experience of being genuinely cared

for. That was on the mother's side, and the babies, on their side, had to totally rely on their mothers, and so had a strong emotional bond. Every human being from the time of birth has that seed of compassion. Eventually we grow up; our brain develops, knowledge develops, and a more sophisticated mind develops. With that, aggressiveness also increases. However, I think that even when the brain develops with an extreme self-centeredness, the person is not blinded. In reality, if you receive more of a sense of concern from others, you will still benefit. I tell people that the concepts of compassion and forgiveness should not be considered religious teachings. Also I say that these qualities should not be considered only good for others, and not necessarily good for yourself. It would be a mistake to

We are very happy that His Holiness is visiting us here.
(literal translation)

think that, because the actual benefit of compassion first goes to the practitioner, and this happens immediately. When you practice compassion, you immediately get more inner peace and more inner strength, and as a result it is much easier to communicate with others. You can even solve problems more easily and more realistically, because the compassionate mind brings calm mind. Calm mind is the basis of proper functioning of the brain. It enables us to judge what's right or what's wrong, and to understand short-term consequences and long-term consequences. When fear, hatred, and jealousy dominate your mind, then the best part of your brain, the part that can judge, cannot function properly. When your mind is dominated by destructive emotions, any decision that you take

When you practice compassion, you immediately get more inner peace and more inner strength, and as a result it is much easier to communicate with others.

becomes unrealistic, and you will never get a satisfactory result. I think that is an important fact. What could be more important? For people with religious faith, harmony among all the different religious traditions is extremely important. In the twenty-first century material development is emphasized, but even in such circumstances the various religious traditions have an important role. From the Buddhist viewpoint, if religion became just a trouble-maker, then it would be of no use, and we would have the right to abandon all religions. But that is not the case. I think the various religions bring immense benefit to millions of people, and religion is still helpful to humanity. At the same time, conflict is taking place in the name of religion, and divisions continue to arise. What are we to do?

How can we keep our religions and in the meantime reduce conflicts in the name of religion? I think that the key is to create harmony on the basis of mutual respect, even mutual admiration. How to do that? Firstly, among all major religious traditions, there are some fundamental differences in the philosophical field. For example, in theistic religions there is a fundamental belief in a creator, and in nontheistic religions there is no such belief. From the viewpoint of theistic religions, the nontheistic religions actually promote some kind of atheism. Those are big differences. Nevertheless, if you look at the practical side of different religions, you will find that they are the same! They all practice love, compassion, forgiveness, tolerance, contentment, and self-discipline. All religions are the

When fear, hatred, and jealousy dominate your mind, then the best part of your brain, the part that can judge, cannot function properly. When your mind is dominated by destructive emotions, any decision that you take becomes unrealistic, and you will never get a satisfactory result. I think that is an important fact. What could be more important?

same, although they may be presented differently because of different philosophies, but they are all the same in practice. Among my friends are some Christians, some Muslims, some Hindus, and some Jews. The individuals are really, really remarkable, and their practice is admirable. For example, I once visited a monastery in Barcelona, Spain, where I met a Christian monk. Before the meeting, the organizers told me that the monk had spent five years in the mountain behind the monastery, living on bread and water. When I met him, his body was weak; he was quite small, and bearded, and his English was even worse than mine. My English was very broken, but compared to him I was fluent. Because of this I had the courage to speak with him in my broken English, and

I asked him, "I heard you spent five years in the mountains as a hermit. What kind is your practice?" Without hesitation he responded to me, "Meditate on love." When he said that, something appeared in his eyes, a kind of light, something special. A similar thing happened when I later met Mother Theresa. Her life was totally dedicated to the welfare of other people, especially the poor people of Calcutta. I visited her organization there, and, oh, it was really wonderful! These are products of Christianity. I also met an American Trappist monk, the late Thomas Merton, and he was a wonderful person. I have met quite a number of such people who through Christian practice became like that. This shows us that different religions have the same potential to produce good human beings

through the practice of love and compassion. At the practice level, all major religions have the same potential and the same message, and there is sufficient reason to respect them. For this reason and with this belief, I started a kind of pilgrimage with a group of people from different faiths. We journeyed to different holy places and sacred sites, and at each place we prayed together, if possible, and if not we did silent meditation. I myself visited two or three times in Jerusalem. From a purely Buddhist viewpoint, I have nothing to do with Jerusalem, but I visited Jerusalem in order to show my respect and admiration of the Abrahamic traditions and also to show other people the oneness of all the major religions. The first time I went to Jerusalem with a Jewish friend and the second time with

I turned back and saw that small Mary statue actually smile. She was just smiling. I had had this kind of experience one time in India with a Tibetan statue of a Tibetan lama, so when I turned back to the statue in Fatima it was a similar experience.

some Hindus. I think also that some Hindus, Christians, Jews, and Muslims have gone there together. Such pilgrimages are very useful to develop a deeper experience of the value of other traditions. Similarly, I visited Lourdes in southern France, and there I stood in front of the statue of Mary and some water pipes. As I stood there, I had a kind of strange, very very deep experience. At that place, millions of people throughout the centuries have received deep inspiration and satisfaction in the name of Jesus Christ, or in the name of Mary. These pilgrims have included sick people who came away with stories of cure or healing. In the same way, at a holy place in Fatima I meditated before a small statue of Mary. After meditating silently for a few minutes, my group began to leave. For a moment I turned back and saw that small Mary statue actually smile. She was just smiling. I had had this kind of experience one time in India with a Tibetan statue of a Tibetan lama, so when I turned back to the statue in Fatima it was a similar experience. Hopefully, there is not something wrong with my head—but I don't know [laughter]. We need further investigation to determine whether something that happens is true or not. Still, I did really get the impression that Mary smiled at me. I feel very happy, because I think that perhaps Mary acknowledged my sincere admiration of what Christianity is about. That is the way it is when we can see the purpose of a different philosophy. One person might say there is God, while another person does not mention God, but

Different religions have the same potential to produce good human beings through the practice of love and compassion. At the practice level, all major religions have the same potential and the same message, and there is sufficient reason to respect them.

talks about self-reliance. Both have the same effect, which is a strong feeling of intimacy and connection with the divine. To some people, the concept of God as creator, the idea that this very life is created by God, brings devotion, and the person feels closer to God. What is the meaning that God teaches us? We are taught, "Love God and love your fellow human being." If you really love God, then you must follow God's wish, and I don't think God's wish is that his followers create more trouble, whether they are Christians, or Muslims, or Hindus, or Jews. I don't think so. I believe that if people actually create trouble among humankind, then their professed love of God is questionable. At different times and in different places, different spiritual masters come. They come out of compassion, out

of a sense of concern and out of love, and they preach many wonderful doctrines. It is clear that their main aim and purpose is to help humanity—not to create human suffering but to reduce suffering. This is very clear. Therefore, tolerance and harmony among all the different religions is extremely important. Look at reality, and then investigate further, and you will get the full conviction that all of the different religious traditions are helpful to humanity. Among humanity there are so many different varieties of people that we need a variety of approaches to achieve the same goal. That goal is compassionate humanity and compassionate human society. As I mentioned earlier, even individuals who do not have much interest in religion still want basic human values. Irrespective of

whether they are believers or nonbelievers, it is important for them to have a happier life and a happier family. That's what I believe, and that's my message. If you feel that it is okay, then take it more seriously. If you don't, then just get up and leave. It's not necessary to carry it home with you. I want to thank the Woodstock town supervisor, and I especially appreciate his making the effort to say a few words in Tibetan. I thank the large number of people who came here because of the situation in Tibet, and who are carrying that banner that says, "Tibet lives in the hearts of Woodstock." I very much appreciate it, because now we are passing through a very difficult period, and we need more moral support from you.

...there is a certain emotional element that bonds us together—that creates the bond between individuals, between mother and child, and between the community and individuals. If a person neglects these things, they will eventually suffer, and suffer a lot.

Among humanity there are so many different varieties of people that we need a variety of approaches to achieve the same goal. That goal is compassionate humanity and compassionate human society. That's what I believe, and that's my message.

A Long Life Prayer for
His Holiness the Dalai Lama

In the land encircled by snow mountains,
You are the source of all happiness
and good;
All-Powerful Chenrezik, Tenzin Gyatso,
Please remain until samsara ends.

Acknowledgments

We wish to express our extraordinary gratitiude and appreciation to His Holiness the Dalai Lama for visiting Woodstock. We hope this little book will celebrate the feeling of warmth and openness characteristic of the town, especially apparent on that day.

We would like to offer our sincere thanks to Tashi Wangdi and the Office of Tibet, and to Jeremy Wilber and the Town of Woodstock. We also express our appreciation to Michael Lang for the Woodstock dove logo and to the photographers Robert Hansen-Sturm of Storm Photo Inc. and Andrea Barrist Stern for the beautiful photographs. Our thanks to Travis Desell for transcribing His Holiness' talk, to Sally Clay for editing, to Jigme Nyima for copy-editing, to Michele Martin, Lama Kathy Wesley, Naomi Schmidt, and Ken Dusyn. We also want to thank the townspeople of Woodstock for helping to make September 21, 2006 a beautiful and memorable day.

Maureen McNicholas and Peter van Deurzen
KTD Publications, Woodstock, New York

Resources

For Information on His Holiness the Dalai Lama's
Activities and Teachings:

The Office of His Holiness the Dalai Lama
Dharamsala, India
www.dalailama.com

The Office of Tibet, New York
The Official Agency of His Holiness the Dalai Lama and
the Tibetan Government-in-Exile to the Americas
www.tibetoffice.org

The Tibetan Youth Development Program
For information contact the Office of Tibet in New York
www.tibetoffice.org

For information about the Town of Woodstock:

Town of Woodstock, Colony of the Arts
Woodstock, New York
www.woodstockny.org

May All Beings Be Happy

The sale of this book helps to support The Tibetan Youth Development Program,
a part of The Tibetan Community Development in North America, to be established in 2007
under the guidance of the Representative of His Holiness the Dalai Lama for North America.